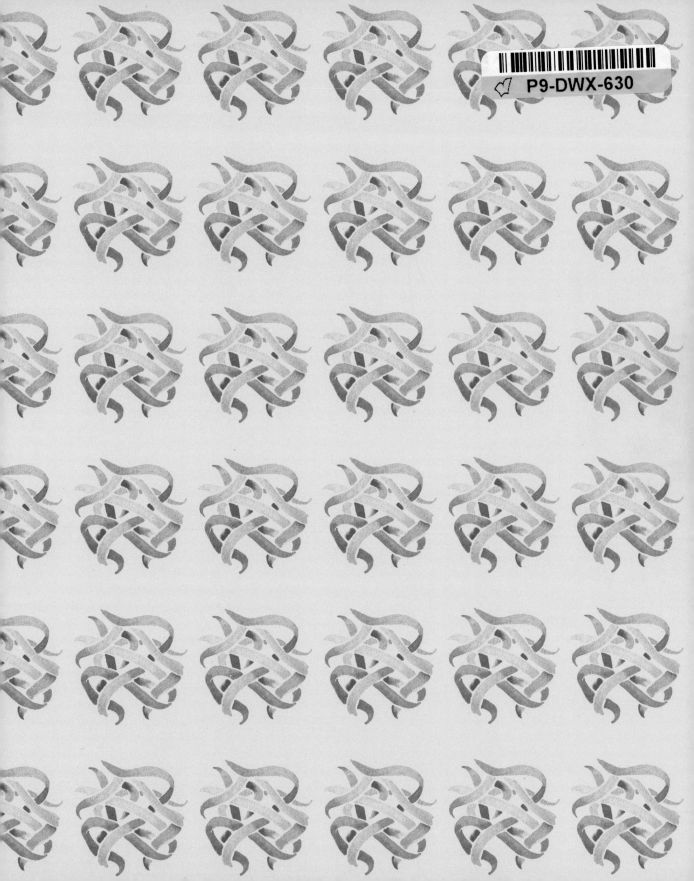

ínspirations

RIBBONS

Over 20 decorative projects for the home

inspirations

RIBBONS

Over 20 decorative projects for the home

LISA BROWN

PHOTOGRAPHY BY LUCINDA SYMONS

LORENZ BOOKS

First published in 1999 by Lorenz Books

Lorenz Books is an imprint of
Anness Publishing Limited
Hermes House
88–89 Blackfriars Road
London SE1 8HA

Published in the USA by Lorenz Books
Anness Publishing Inc., 27 West 20th Street
New York, NY 10011; (800) 354–9657

Distributed in Canada by Raincoast Books
8680 Cambie Street, Vancouver, British Columbia V6P 6M9

A CIP catalogue record for this book is available from the British Library

ISBN 0 7548 0187 X

Publisher: Joanna Lorenz
Editor: Sarah Ainley
Copy Editor: Beverley Jollands
Editorial Reader: Joy Wotton
Designer: Lilian Lindblom
Step Photography: Rodney Forte
Styled Photography: Lucinda Symons
Stylist: Lisa Brown
Illustrators: Madeleine David and Robert Highton
Production Controller: Karina Han

Printed in Hong Kong/China

1 3 5 7 9 10 8 6 4 2

CONTENTS

INTRODUCTION

Until quite recently, ribbons seemed to have been relegated to decorating Christmas and birthdays gifts. Whether a length of old velvet or metallic ribbon, the choice was not very inspiring. Now, however, ribbons are making a big comeback, with a wide variety of colours, designs, materials and sizes available for you to buy even from non-specialist shops.

I have to admit to a small passion for ribbons, buying lengths without any particular purpose for them in mind, but simply because I have been attracted to a colour or pattern. I once spent a happy half-hour deliberating over a stack of old ribbon on a market stall in France, eventually choosing five beautiful reels. This book is therefore the saviour of my ribbon box, with over 20 fabulously creative ideas for using ribbons. There are classic and new ideas for wrapping gifts – of course – but also for creating a headboard, cushion, lampshade and even a wind chime. Other ideas are decorative rather than functional, including two inspired by summer fêtes: a row of miniature flags like bunting and a strip of ribbon decorated with looped rosettes. My own particular favourite idea is for making shelf trims from ribbon.

As well as beautiful photographs of the finished items, each project is clearly shown step by step, so that you see everything you need to make it and exactly what to do at each stage. The range of materials and the equipment you might need to work on the projects is detailed at the back of the book, together with a useful section covering basic techniques, such as how to tie the perfect bow, weaving ribbon, and making ribbon roses.

Deborah Barker

TASSELLED TIE-BACK

Shocking pink ribbons in a variety of styles make up this pretty tie-back. Satin ribbon is ruched on to a band to hold the curtain in place, while the tassel hangs decoratively to one side. Wire-edged ribbons give the tassel shape and volume.

YOU WILL NEED
large-eyed tapestry needle
narrow embroidery ribbon
wooden beads in two sizes
scissors
selection of satin, velvet and wire-edged ribbons
needle and strong thread
2 brass rings

1 Using a large-eyed tapestry needle, thread narrow embroidery ribbon around two large wooden beads to make the tassel head.

2 When the beads are completely covered, tie off the ends securely. Create a hanging loop at the top of the smaller bead.

3 To make a rosette, cut a length of satin ribbon and join the ends neatly together, turning in the raw edges. Work a running stitch along both edges of the ribbon.

4 Gather up the edges tightly to make a puff shape and secure the threads. Make a second rosette, using ribbon of a different width and colour.

5 To make a loop rosette, cut two lengths of narrow velvet ribbon. Fold the ends to the centre of the first length and secure with a stitch.

6 Add the second loop at right angles and secure all the layers through the centre.

9

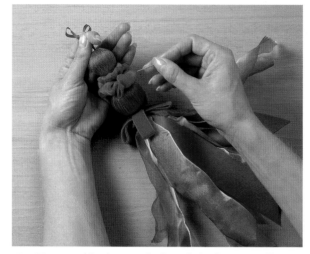

7 Select satin and wire-edged ribbons for the skirt of the tassel, cutting them to twice the finished length: this will depend on the size of the tassel head, so experiment until the tassel looks right. Arrange the ribbons in a star shape and secure by stitching through all the layers in the centre.

8 To assemble the tassel, thread the large needle with several lengths of strong thread and stitch through the centre of each element, starting with the skirt. Fasten off securely when you reach the top of the smaller bead.

9 To make the tie-back, cut a suitable length of wide satin ribbon. Neaten the raw edges and stitch a brass ring securely to each end. Cut a second piece of the same ribbon twice the length of the tie-back and gather by working a line of running stitches along the centre.

10 Draw up the fullness to fit the foundation ribbon and stitch down the centre. Sew the tassel's hanging loop to one end of the tie-back, so that it will hang at the side of the curtain.

ROSETTE PICTURE HANGING

Learning how to make a rosette is a must for ribbon enthusiasts. Rosettes have many uses, but they always look striking as part of a decorative picture hanging. The elegant colour scheme of black, grey and white enhances this monochromatic arrangement.

YOU WILL NEED
tapestry canvas
pair of compasses (compass)
permanent marker (felt-tip) pen
ruler
scissors
15 mm/⅝ in petersham or grosgrain ribbon in black
needle and strong thread
20 mm/¾ in petersham or grosgrain ribbons in grey and off-white
wide striped petersham or grosgrain ribbon

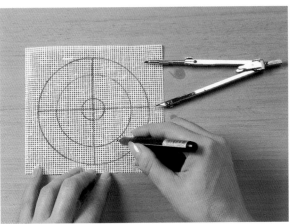

1 Decide on the size of the rosette then draw a circle slightly smaller than this on the canvas, using compasses (a compass) and a permanent marker (felt-tip) pen. Draw vertical and horizontal guidelines through the centre and smaller circles to act as guides for placing the loops of the rosette. Cut out.

2 To make the centre of the rosette, cut a length of the narrow black ribbon. Fold the ribbon at an angle of about 30° in the centre.

3 Fold the right-hand piece of ribbon over the left-hand piece.

▶

13

4 Repeat, always folding the right-hand piece of ribbon over the left-hand piece.

5 You will eventually form a six-sided button shape. Tuck the ends inside at the back and secure with a couple of stitches.

6 Cut enough equal lengths of grey ribbon to fit all round the outer ring of the rosette and fold each in half. Using the first circle as a guide, stitch the loops to the backing canvas.

7 Use narrower black ribbon for the second row and attach as before, arranging the loops inside the first circle.

8 Make a third circle using off-white ribbon and overlapping the ends of the loops in the centre.

9 Stitch the black ribbon centre in place, covering the ends of the white loops.

10 Cut a length of wide striped ribbon for the tail and fold the ends into points. Stitch the raw edges together to secure. Fold the ribbon in half at an angle and stitch to the back of the rosette.

Hang the rosette from a length of wide black ribbon. Trim the end into a fishtail.

SPECIAL OCCASION TABLE

Dressing the table for a wedding or a birthday party can be daunting, but it is very easy to make a big difference with ribbon. This eye-catching design uses exuberant multicoloured gingham bows, which are attached to each corner of a white cloth with a matching hem.

YOU WILL NEED
large piece of coloured cotton fabric
tape measure
iron
scissors
dressmaker's pins
sewing machine
matching thread
white cotton fabric
50 mm/2 in wide wire-edged gingham
ribbon in yellow, blue and red
florist's reel wire
needle

1 Fold and press a 5 cm/2 in wide double hem around all four sides of the coloured fabric to be used as the undercloth.

2 Unfold the hem again and trim diagonally across each corner to reduce some of the bulk from the fabric.

3 Refold the hem as before and pin in place.

4 Tuck in the edge of the topmost fold to make a mock mitre at each corner. Pin in place, then machine stitch close to the inner edge of the hem using matching thread.

5 For the white overcloth, press a small single hem to the right side around all four edges and tuck in the folded corners to make mock mitres.

6 Pin a length of wide gingham ribbon over the hem, covering the raw edges of the fabric.

7 At the corner, take the gingham ribbon slightly beyond the edge of the fabric, then fold it back on itself as shown, to form a neat mitre.

8 Pin the ribbon all the way around the cloth, then machine stitch in place along both edges.

9 To make a bow for each corner, cut a 1 m/1 yd length from each of the three coloured ribbons. Loop each ribbon over on itself and pinch together firmly with your fingers at the centre.

10 Place all the ribbon loops together and bind them tightly at the centre, using a length of florist's reel wire.

11 To make the tails of the bows, cut another 1 m/ 1 yd piece from each colour and trim each end into a fishtail. Bind the centres of the tails together with wire, then bind to the bow. Fluff out the ribbon loops to make a frothy bow and stitch or pin it to the corner of the table-cloth when it is on the table.

RIBBON DOOR CURTAIN

Let fresh air in and keep flies out with a brilliant Mexican-style curtain made from colourful
satin ribbon. Each length is finished with a large glass bead to add weight and substance.
The number of lengths you need will depend on the width of the door frame.

YOU WILL NEED
measuring tape
25 mm/1 in square softwood batten
hacksaw
electric drill
ruler
pencil
15 mm/⅝ in wide double-faced satin ribbon in six bright colours
scissors
coloured glass disc-shaped beads
staple gun
2 woodscrews
screwdriver

1 Measure your door frame. Cut a length of batten to fit snugly inside the top of the door frame.

2 Drill a small hole about 1.5 cm/⅝ in from each end of the batten to hold the screws. ▶

3 Draw a pencil line along the centre of the batten, then mark off every 2.5 cm/1 in to indicate the positions for attaching the ribbon.

4 Cut a length of satin ribbon for each point marked on the batten, about 15 cm/6 in longer than the door measurement to allow for attachment and tying on the glass beads. Trim one end of each length into neat points.

5 Fold the trimmed end over for about 10 cm/4 in, then push the folded end through the hole in the centre of a glass bead. Pull the whole length of the ribbon through the loop and pull taut to hold the bead securely. Repeat with all the ribbon lengths.

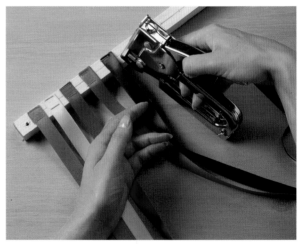

6 Fold under about 1.5 cm/⅝ in at the other end of each length of ribbon and staple to the softwood batten at a pencil mark. It is easier to do this on a large table or on the floor, but check that the ribbons are the same length as you go. Follow the same colour sequence all across the curtain. Finally, attach the batten to the door frame with two long woodscrews.

PILLOWCASE EDGINGS

Glamorize plain bedlinen by edging a pile of pillows with ribbon bands and bows.
Bright ginghams work beautifully in a child's bedroom, but you could adapt the idea
using cooler colours for a more sophisticated look.

YOU WILL NEED
plain white cotton pillowcases
plain and gingham ribbons of various widths
tape measure
scissors
fusible bonding web
iron
needle and matching thread
dressmaker's pins

1 For the banded pillowcase, cut lengths of three different ribbons about 5 cm/2 in longer than the width of the pillowcase. Cut three lengths of fusible bonding web to size and use to attach each of the ribbons.

2 Turn in the raw edges and stitch the ribbons to the pillowcase at each end. Handsew with tiny stitches along each long edge of the pillowcase.

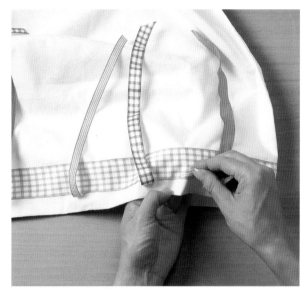

3 For the pillowcase with ties, cut two 30 cm/ 12 in lengths from each of the five different narrow ribbons and pin one of each pair at regular intervals along the folded edge of the pillowcase opening. Stitch in place.

4 Using fusible bonding web, attach a length of wide ribbon to cover the ends of the ties. Hand or machine stitch around all the edges to secure.

5 Attach the matching ribbon lengths to the other side of the pillowcase opening, folding in the raw edges and stitching neatly to secure.

6 To decorate the pillowcase with ties, cut lengths of ribbon of differing widths and pin across the corners. Slip stitch to secure. ▶

7 Fold the raw edges of the ribbons over on to the underside of the pillowcase. Cut a second length of each ribbon, fold in the ends to conceal the raw edges and slip stitch in place.

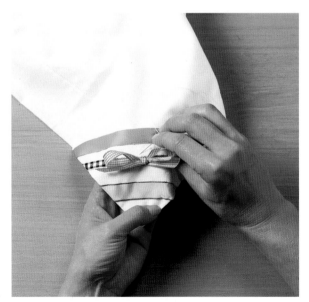

8 Finish the corner with a small ribbon bow, stitched through the knot to prevent it from coming undone.

DRESSED-UP COAT HANGERS

Give your prettiest clothes the care they deserve with padded satin coat hangers.
These luxurious hangers have been decorated with roses and bows made with small quantities
of exquisite silk and embroidered ribbons in beautiful, muted colours.

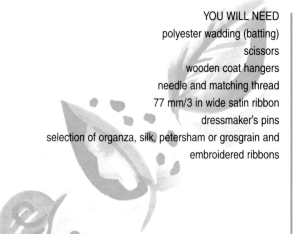

YOU WILL NEED
polyester wadding (batting)
scissors
wooden coat hangers
needle and matching thread
77 mm/3 in wide satin ribbon
dressmaker's pins
selection of organza, silk, petersham or grosgrain and
embroidered ribbons

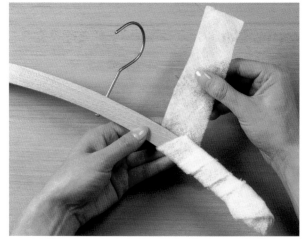

1 Cut a strip of polyester wadding (batting) for each of the coat hangers. Wind it around and secure with a few stitches.

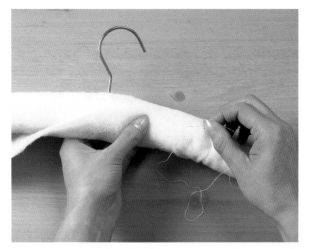

2 Cut a rectangle of wadding to cover the prepared hanger and stitch neatly, trimming and tucking in the ends.

3 Cut two lengths of wide satin ribbon to make the cover for the hanger and, with right sides together, stitch each end in a gentle curve.

4 Stitch along one long edge of the satin cover and turn to the right side.

5 Fit the cover over the hanger and slip stitch the top edges neatly, gathering the ends gently and easing in the fullness as you sew.

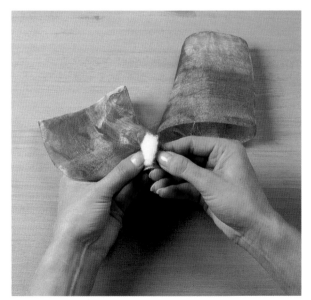

6 To make a rose to decorate the hanger, fold a tiny piece of wadding into the end of a length of organza ribbon and secure with a stitch.

7 Fold and wind the rest of the ribbon around this central bud, stitching through the layers to secure. Tuck in the raw edge and stitch down. Make two roses for each hanger. ▶

8 To make a rosette, cut a length of silk ribbon about five times its width and join the raw edges.

9 Gather the ribbon with a running stitch slightly above the centre. Pull up and secure. Flatten the ribbon out with your fingers to complete the rosette. Make two for each hanger.

10 To make a leaf, take a small piece of green petersham or grosgrain ribbon and fold both ends down to the side. Work a running stitch along this side and pull up the gathers tightly, securing with a stitch. Make four for each hanger.

11 Tie a length of embroidered ribbon around the centre of each hanger to finish in a bow around the hook. Use this as a foundation to attach the roses, leaves and rosettes. Add loops of ribbon to make a pleasing arrangement.

TRINKET BAG

Join together vertical lengths of Fortuny-style pleated ribbon to make up a sculptural trinket or evening bag. Line with a complementary iridescent fabric and embellish with sparkling beads along the top edge as a pretty finishing touch.

YOU WILL NEED
1.6 m/1⅞ yd pleated wire-edged ribbon, 50 mm/2 in wide

scissors

tape measure

dressmaker's pins

needle and matching thread

40 cm/16 in pleated wire-edged ribbon, 56 mm/2¼ in wide

matching organza fabric

plate

pencil

sewing machine

38 cm/15 in fine matching cord

glass beads

1 To make the side of the bag, cut eight pieces of ribbon 20 cm/8 in long and oversew the pieces together in a circle.

2 For the bottom of the bag, stitch the two ends of the other ribbon together.

3 Run a gathering stitch along one side of the ribbon, pull up and secure.

4 Slip stitch the outer edge of the bottom of the bag to the lower edge of the side, turning in the raw edges.

5 For the lining, cut a rectangle 18 x 40 cm/7 x 16 in and a circle with a 7 cm/2¾ in radius from the organza, using a plate.

6 Machine stitch the side seam, and pin and tack the side to the bottom of the bag. Machine stitch together.

7 Fit the lining into the bag. Fold in the top edges of both the lining and the outer fabric and slip stitch the two together.

8 To make the carriers for the tie, cut two 6 cm/2½ in lengths of cord and poke the raw ends through a side seam on either side of the bag, 4 cm/1½ in from the top. Stitch in place. Cut a piece of cord 25 cm/10 in long, fold it in half and knot the ends. Thread the loop through the carriers and pass the knotted ends through the loop.

Luxurious ribbon fabrics in sumptuous colours help make an exquisite accessory.

9 Hand stitch decorative glass beads around the top edge of the bag at regular intervals.

EASTER WREATH

Whether it's a simple circle of twigs or a lavish floral creation, ribbons will always enhance a decorative wreath. This delicate wreath for Easter is wired with artificial birds' eggs and tied with diaphanous bows of organza ribbon.

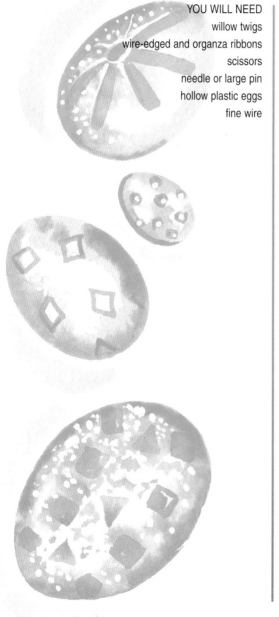

YOU WILL NEED
willow twigs
wire-edged and organza ribbons
scissors
needle or large pin
hollow plastic eggs
fine wire

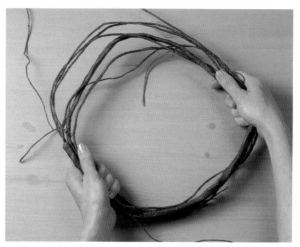

1 Soak the willow twigs in lukewarm water to soften them and carefully bend a group of five or six long twigs into a circle.

2 Continue adding twigs to the circle, intertwining the ends and overlocking them with shorter twigs to create a firm wreath structure.

3 Loop a length of wire-edged ribbon around the wreath, then tie in a bow. Use this loop to hang the wreath on the door or wall.

4 Cut several lengths of organza ribbon and tie into bows or knots around the wreath. Trim the ends into neat fishtails.

5 Using a needle or a large pin, gently pierce a hole in each end of each egg and carefully feed a length of fine wire through the holes.

6 Position the eggs around the wreath and tie in place. Trim the excess wire.

CHRISTMAS DECORATIONS

Bright multicoloured ribbon decorations make a change from traditional red and gold at Christmas. Apply them to golden chocolate coins, luxurious buttons and sumptuous organza roses for an eye-catching display on your Christmas tree.

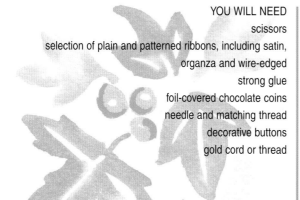

YOU WILL NEED
scissors
selection of plain and patterned ribbons, including satin, organza and wire-edged
strong glue
foil-covered chocolate coins
needle and matching thread
decorative buttons
gold cord or thread

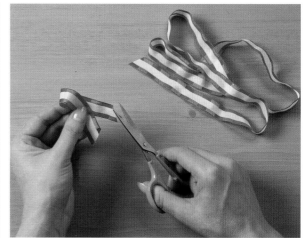

1 To make a medal, cut a short length of narrow ribbon and fold it in half. Trim each end of ribbon to form a point.

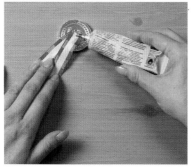

2 Glue the folded ribbon to the back of a large foil-covered chocolate coin.

3 Cut a length of wider ribbon for the chocolate coin to hang from, adding a second, narrower piece if you wish. Fold in half and stick the ends to the coin. Glue on a second coin to conceal the raw edges.

4 To make a rosette, gather a length of satin ribbon along one edge and draw up tightly. Join the raw edges neatly.

5 Make a rose from a length of organza ribbon by folding it lengthways and winding it around itself, stitching at the base to secure.

6 Cut tails from wire-edged ribbon as for the medal, and add a loop of ribbon for the top.

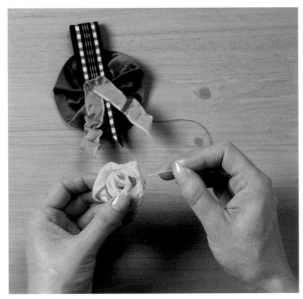

7 Stitch both ribbons to the rosette and sew the rose in the centre to complete the decoration.

8 For the large rosette, cut two equal lengths of wide ribbon and fold the ends to the middle of each. Place at right angles to each other and stitch the centres together. ▶

9 Stitch together two loops of narrow wire-edged ribbon in the same way and attach them diagonally to the first cross. Add a decorative button in the centre.

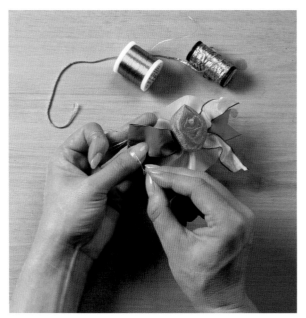

10 Make a hanging loop of gold cord or thread for each decoration and stitch in place.

WOVEN HEADBOARD

Ribbon is an ideal material for weaving, and wonderful effects can be achieved with subtle combinations of colour and texture. This headboard sets the tone for a minimalist Japanese-style bedroom in neutral shades.

YOU WILL NEED
25 mm/1 in square softwood batten
hacksaw
sandpaper
electric drill and bit
tape measure
pencil
wood glue
dowels
4 right-angled fixing brackets
screws
screwdriver
5 m/5½ yd each grosgrain ribbon in blue,
brown and beige, 12 mm/½ in wide
20 m/22 yd cream satin or taffeta ribbon,
25 mm/1 in wide
5 m/5½ yd each satin striped ribbon in blue,
brown and beige
5 m/5½ yd each grosgrain ribbon in blue,
brown and beige, 15 mm/⅝ in wide
scissors
staple gun

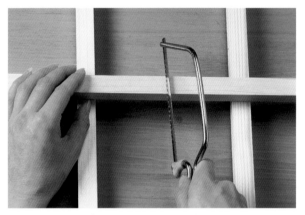

1 Cut the softwood batten into four lengths, each measuring 90 cm/36 in. This will make a headboard to fit a single bed. Sand the cut edges.

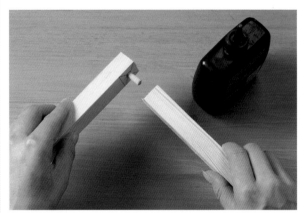

2 Using an electric drill with a bit to fit the dowels, make a hole in each end of the two battens that will form the horizontal pieces of the frame. In each of the two side pieces, drill a hole about 1 cm/½ in from the top and a second hole 60 cm/24 in down. Use wood glue to secure the dowel joints and complete the frame. Allow the glue to dry. ▶

3 Screw four right-angled fixing brackets to the reverse side of the headboard frame to reinforce the joints and hold the frame rigid while you work. This will help to keep the woven pattern symmetrical.

4 Cut a selection of ribbons into 70 cm/28 in lengths. Lay them vertically on the frame to plan the pattern, making sure that it is symmetrical. Begin at the centre with a wide piece of grosgrain overlaid with a lighter coloured satin stripe ribbon, then work outwards with alternate narrower satin and grosgrain ribbons. Repeat the sequence until you have filled the width of the frame. Use a staple gun to attach the ribbon to the frame, pulling each piece taut.

5 Cut two short pieces of cream satin or taffeta ribbon and staple to cover the wooden batten at the top two corners.

6 Interweave ribbons horizontally across the head-board in a pattern sequence similar to the warp. Turn the headboard over and staple the raw ends securely to the frame as before, making sure that the ribbons are pulled quite taut.

DECK-CHAIR COVER

An old deck-chair can be transformed with a new cover, and an interesting way to make this is with strong grosgrain ribbon. Here, two boldly contrasting colours have been woven together to achieve a striking checkerboard effect.

YOU WILL NEED
deck-chair
claw hammer, pliers or screwdriver
large sheet of cardboard or scrap timber
tape measure
pencil
39 mm/1½ in wide grosgrain ribbon in white and blue
(10 m/10 yd is sufficient for a small chair)
scissors
drawing pins (thumb tacks)
dressmaker's pins
needle and tacking (basting) thread
sewing machine
matching thread
staple gun

1 Remove the old canvas from the chair frame, retaining it to use as a size guide for the new cover, then carefully prise out any old nails or fixings.

2 Mark the dimensions of the cover on a large sheet of cardboard or timber. Cut lengths of white grosgrain ribbon to the length of the measured rectangle, plus about 10 cm/4 in for fixing. Pin the ribbons to the board side by side along the top of the rectangle to form the "warp".

3 Cut lengths of blue ribbon to fit across the rectangle and form the "weft". To weave the cover, pin a blue ribbon to the warp length at one side, weave it under and over the warp until you reach the other side, then pin securely again. Repeat until you have the size required.

4 Tack (baste) across the upper and lower edges of the weaving to hold the warp in place.

5 Cut two lengths of blue ribbon to fit down each side of the new cover. Lay one length over the raw edges of the weft at each side and tack in position. Remove the cover from the board and machine stitch the blue and white side ribbons together, stitching very close to both edges.

6 Attach the new cover to the wooden frame by wrapping the ends of the ribbons around the horizontal rungs and stapling securely in place.

RIBBON WIND CHIME

The delicate sound of a wind chime on a breezy summer evening is always a pleasure.
Make your own using lengths of medium-width ribbon tied to pieces of silvery piping.
Finish with washers at each end and let the wind do the rest.

YOU WILL NEED
13 cm/5 in diameter flush lampshade ring
newspaper
metallic silver spray paint
ruler
vice (optional)
hacksaw
2.1 m/7 ft chrome-plated piping, 15 mm/⅝ in diameter
sandpaper
electric drill and bit
5 m/5½ yd navy grosgrain ribbon, 5 mm/¼ in wide
scissors
20 small silver beads with large holes
4 m/4½ yd navy double-faced satin ribbon, 15 mm/⅝ in wide
20 metal washers, 2.5 cm/1 in diameter
needle and matching thread
4 long silver beads

1 Place the lampshade ring on a sheet of newspaper and spray with metallic silver paint. Leave to dry, then turn the ring over and spray the other side.

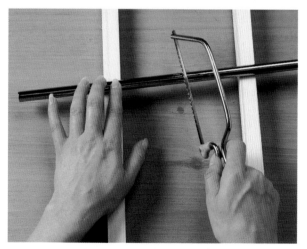

2 Use a hacksaw to saw the piping into ten 20 cm/ 8 in lengths. A vice can be used to hold the piping as you cut. Smooth any sharp edges with sandpaper.

46

3 Drill a small hole through one end of each length of piping.

4 Cut ten 30 cm/12 in lengths from the grosgrain ribbon and thread one through the hole at the top of each length of pipe.

5 Pull the ends of the ribbon until they are level and thread two small silver beads on to each doubled length.

6 Tie the ends of the ribbon in a knot around the lampshade ring and trim the raw edges into neat points. When all the ribbons are tied on the ring, slide one of the silver beads up to the top to hold each ribbon securely.

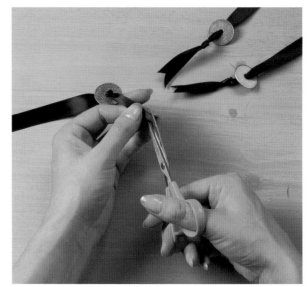

7 Cut ten 30 cm/12 in lengths of the satin ribbon. Thread one end of each through a metal washer and tie in a knot about 5 cm/2 in from the end.

8 Fold the end of each ribbon in half and trim into a neat fishtail with a pair of scissors.

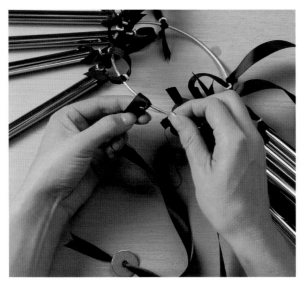

9 Fold the untrimmed end of each satin ribbon over the lampshade ring between two chimes. The ribbon should be just long enough for the washer to strike the chimes at the base. Turn in the raw edge and stitch the satin ribbon in place securely using matching thread.

10 Cut the remaining grosgrain ribbon into four 50 cm/20 in lengths. Tie these at quarter positions around the ring, then tie the other ends together in a secure knot. Thread a long silver bead on to each hanging end.

RIBBON-BOUND STATIONERY

In the past, ribbon was used for holding together important documents, which were often finished with a seal. Echo its historical role by making a gift of stationery tied with wire-edged ribbon, or make a menu or invitation more interesting with a ribbon and seal.

YOU WILL NEED
mounting board
craft knife
steel rule
cutting mat
handmade paper
spray adhesive
1.2 m/1⅓ yd grosgrain ribbon, 39 mm/1½ in wide
scissors
PVA (white) glue
2 m/2¼ yd grosgrain ribbon, 15 mm/⅝ in wide
leatherette paper

1 To make a portfolio for papers or letters, cut two rectangles of mounting board 33 x 26 cm/ 13 x 10¼ in and two rectangles of handmade paper 37 x 28 cm/14½ x 11 in. Carefully spray the paper with adhesive and apply each board flush with one long edge, leaving 2 cm/¾ in turning for the other three sides. Fold in the corners, then the sides.

2 Cut four 8 cm/3¼ in lengths of 39 mm/1½ in ribbon. Using PVA (white) glue, stick each piece diagonally across the covered corners of the boards. Fold over and glue the ends to the underside of the boards.

▶

51

3 Cut two 45 cm/18 in lengths of 15 mm/⅝ in ribbon. Using PVA (white) glue, stick one end of each to the middle of the long covered edges of the boards. Cut the free ends into fishtails. Cut two 32.5 x 25 cm/12¾ x 10 in rectangles of handmade paper and stick centrally to the underside of the boards using spray adhesive.

4 Cut a 35 cm/14 in length of wide ribbon. Using PVA glue, stick this to the right side of the uncovered edge of one board with an overlap of 1.5 cm/⅝ in and an equal turning allowance at each end. Stick the opposite edge of the ribbon to the other board in the same way to make a hinge.

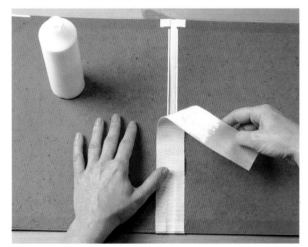

5 Turn the ends of the ribbon to the inside. Cut a 32.5 cm/12¾ in length of wide ribbon and glue it with PVA glue along the inside of the hinge. Following the template at the back of the book, cut two pockets from leatherette paper, using a craft knife, and fold the hems to the right side.

6 Cut two 43.5 cm/17 in lengths of narrow ribbon. Using PVA glue, stick one length of ribbon to the folded edge of each pocket, enclosing the hem. Fold the pockets backwards, following the solid lines of the template, and forwards, following the broken lines. Position the pockets along the outer edges inside the portfolio and stick the tabs in place using PVA glue.

LUXURIOUS GIFTWRAPPING

Beautiful, extravagant ribbon bows and rosettes add true distinction to special gifts.
Choose wrapping paper in interesting textures and subtle colours to complement them,
and try combining ribbons in several different shades for enchanting effects.

YOU WILL NEED
gold wire-edged ribbon in two shades
scissors
organza ribbon in three colours
bead-edged ribbon 5 cm/2 in wide
tape measure
double-sided adhesive tape
gold corded ribbon
thin cardboard
stapler

1 To tie a parcel with gold wire-edged ribbon in two shades, wrap one length of ribbon around the parcel and tie in a single knot on top. Wrap the second length around the parcel in the other direction and tie in a knot at the same position. Hold one end of each knot in each hand and tie all the ends together in a bow. Open out the loops and cut the free ends into fishtails.

2 For a multicoloured bow, place organza ribbons in three colours one on top of the other and tie around the parcel together. Open out the loops and cut the free ends into fishtails. ▶

53

3 To make a pompom, cut a length of bead-edged ribbon 126 cm/49 in long and fold into seven concertina (accordion) pleats, each 18 cm/7 in long. Trim the ribbon ends diagonally. Holding the pleats together, carefully make a 2 cm/¾ in cut in the centre of each long edge.

4 Cut a second length of ribbon long enough to wrap around the parcel plus 15 cm/6 in. Tie this length around the centre of the pleats, then wrap it around the parcel and secure the ends underneath with double-sided adhesive tape. Open out the folds of the pompom to form puffed loops.

5 For a rosette-trimmed parcel, wrap a length of gold, corded ribbon around the parcel and secure underneath with adhesive tape. Cut a 3 cm/1¼ in diameter circle of thin cardboard and a 110 cm/ 43 in length of ribbon. Fold under one end of the ribbon, then make a pleat and staple to the centre of the cardboard.

6 Continue pleating and stapling the ribbon, working outwards around the circle in a spiral. Staple the end of the ribbon under the cardboard. Stick the rosette to the top of the parcel using the adhesive tape.

APPLIQUED CAFE CURTAIN

Using ruched ribbons for appliqué gives an interesting, three-dimensional effect, which can be bold and bright or subtle and delicate, depending on the fabrics and ribbons you use. Here, organza ribbons have been applied in a fine tracery on light voile to make a pretty, airy curtain.

YOU WILL NEED
tape measure
voile
scissors
dressmaker's pins
sewing machine
matching thread
iron
paper for template
pencil
fabric marker
needle
organza ribbons in green and pink

1 Calculate the width and drop of the curtain and cut out the voile, adding 5 cm/2 in to the width and 15 cm/6 in to the length. To make the facing, cut a second piece of voile to the same width by 30 cm/12 in. Turn under and machine stitch a 5 mm/¼ in hem along the lower edge of the facing. Press. With right sides together, pin the facing to the curtain matching the top edges.

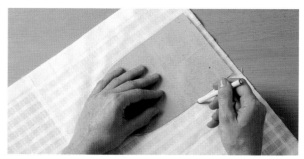

2 Enlarge the scallop template at the back of the book, and cut out of paper. Add the width of the template to the proposed width of each fabric loop (which should be 4–7 cm/1½–2¾ in) and divide the finished curtain width by this figure to calculate the number of scallops required. Allow for a strip at each end of the curtain. Draw around the scallop template along the top of the curtain, using a fabric marker.

3 Machine stitch the facing to the curtain along the marked lines. Cut out the scallops leaving a 1 cm/½ in seam allowance. Clip the corners and into the curves.

4 Turn the curtain through to the right side and press. Top stitch around the top edges, 4 mm/⅛ in from the edge.

5 Turn and press a double hem 1 cm/½ in wide down each side of the curtain. Turn and press a 5 cm/2 in double hem along the bottom.

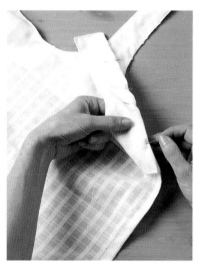

6 Mitre the corners and slip stitch in place. Turn and press a 1 cm/½ in hem down both sides of the facing. Slip stitch the facing and all hems in place.

7 To make the fabric loops, turn 5 cm/2 in of each strip to the back of the curtain and pin and hand stitch to the facing.

8 Cut the green ribbon into 1 m/1 yd lengths. Machine stitch down the centre of each length, gathering the ribbon as you sew, or gently pull the bobbin thread to gather the ribbon. ▶

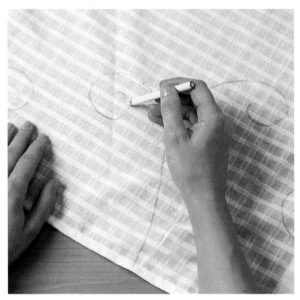

9 Mark out the designs freehand on the curtain, using a fabric marker.

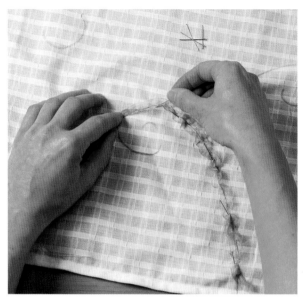

10 Pin the ruched ribbon on to the curtain, following the lines of the design.

11 Machine stitch the ribbon in place along the marked lines, stitching carefully along the gathering thread.

12 Gather the pink ribbon as before and cut a strip 15 cm/6 in long for each flower. Make three small loops in each and pin the flowers to the curtain at random. Machine stitch, securing the loops in place.

FAUX DADO (CHAIR) RAIL

You can give instant sophistication to your hallway using ribbons to create the illusion of panelled walls. Narrow, light-catching satin ribbon has been added to achieve a three-dimensional effect. For the most convincing results, use colours quite close in shade to the wall.

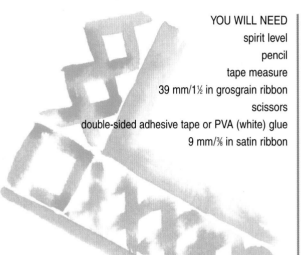

YOU WILL NEED
spirit level
pencil
tape measure
39 mm/1½ in grosgrain ribbon
scissors
double-sided adhesive tape or PVA (white) glue
9 mm/⅜ in satin ribbon

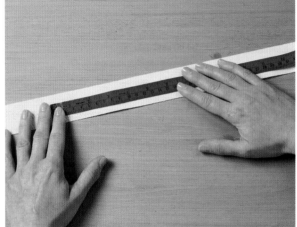

1 Decide on the height of the dado (chair) rail and mark the position on the wall using a spirit level and pencil. Measure the width of the wall and cut a length of grosgrain ribbon to fit.

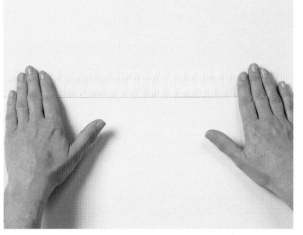

2 Apply double-sided adhesive tape or PVA (white) glue to one side of the ribbon and stick to the wall.

60

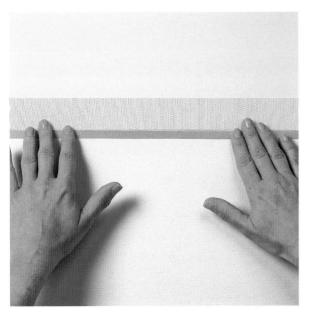

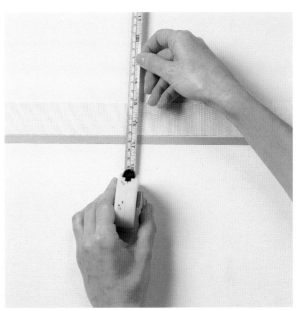

3 Cut a matching length of narrow satin ribbon and glue immediately beneath the first length to create a shaded effect.

4 Measure the area between the dado and the skirting board and plan the positions of the panels. Mark on the wall using the spirit level and pencil.

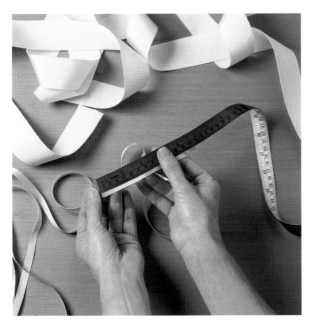

5 Cut four lengths of each ribbon for each panel, a little longer than the finished measurements.

6 Mark the final lengths on the ribbons, then lay them flat on the work surface to enable you to cut the 45° angles accurately.

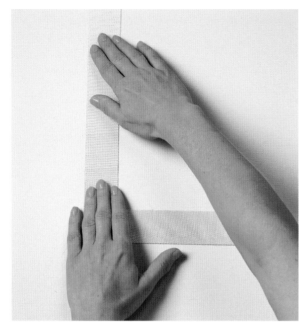

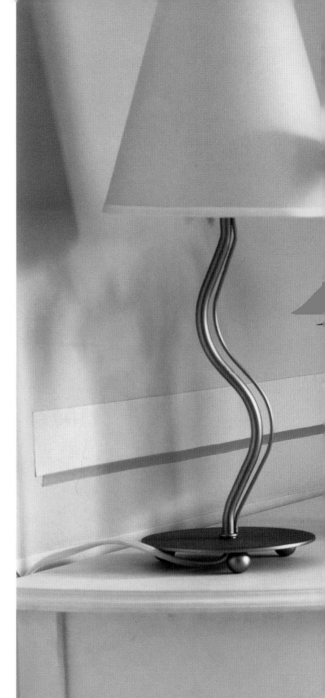

7 Glue the ribbons to the wall, fitting them snugly together at the corners.

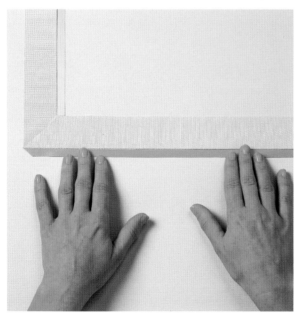

8 Glue the satin ribbons under the horizontal ribbons and to one side of the vertical ribbons to give the effect of solid mouldings.

ROSY LAMPSHADE

It's easy to make ribbon roses and they always look gorgeous. You simply wrap, roll and tweak.

Here, they are randomly applied to a plain lampshade to add splashes of colour.

YOU WILL NEED
wire-edged ribbon in pink and red
tape measure
scissors
needle and matching thread
plain lampshade
strong glue or glue gun
ribbon trim

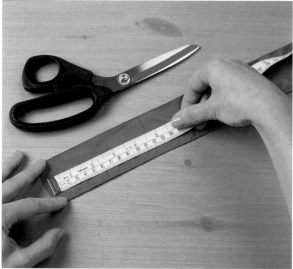

1 Cut a 40 cm/16 in length of wire-edged ribbon for each rose.

2 Find the wire at one side of the ribbon and pull from both ends, ruching the ribbon.

3 Keep pulling until the ribbon is evenly ruched and the wire ends even.

4 Fold the ribbon in half and roll it up loosely, starting at the raw ends.

5 Fan out the ribbon edge to create the rose, and secure the base with a few small slip stitches.

6 Make enough roses to cover the lampshade at random, then glue them on. ▶

7 Using a measuring tape, measure around the base of the lampshade to find the circumference.

8 Cut a piece of ribbon trim to this size, adding a small overlap allowance. Glue the ribbon in place using strong glue or a glue gun.

LINEN THROW

A relatively small amount of expensive ribbon makes a big difference to this natural linen bed or sofa throw. Lengths of antique-style crushed velvet ribbon applied diagonally across the throw bring an element of luxury to the whole setting.

YOU WILL NEED

1.5 m/5 ft square natural linen

fabric marker

ruler

iron

crushed velvet ribbon, 30 mm/1¼ in and 15 mm/⅝ in wide

dressmaker's pins

tape measure

scissors

sewing machine

matching thread

167 cm/5 ft 7 in square silk lining (widths joined if necessary)

needle

1 Lay the linen flat and mark a border all around it, 7 cm/2¾ in from the edge. Press a fold into the fabric diagonally across the centre.

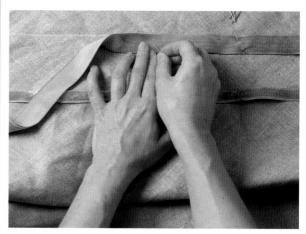

2 Working from the centre outwards, pin lengths of velvet ribbon diagonally across the linen following the direction of the fold and alternating the widths. Use a tape measure to check that the lines are parallel.

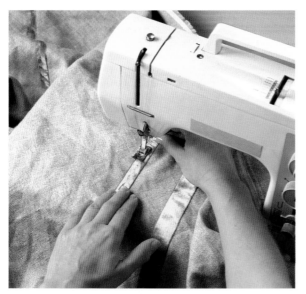

3 Machine stitch the ribbons in place, stitching close to the edges. To ensure that the ribbon lies flat, stitch both edges in the same direction.

4 With right sides together, match two opposite edges of the lining fabric to the border line marked on the linen. Pin and machine stitch the seams, starting and finishing 2 cm/¾ in from each end of the marked lines.

5 Match the two remaining edges in the same way. Machine stitch the edges together, leaving a 30 cm/12 in gap on one side.

6 Turn the fabric through to the right side. Centre the upper fabric to give an even border 7 cm/ 2¾ in wide and press with a warm iron.

▶

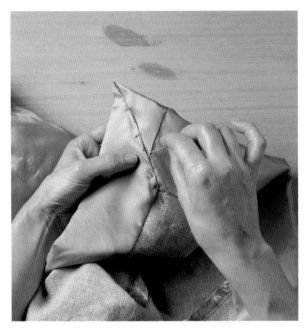

7 Turn in the lining along the opening edge and press. Slip stitch the gap closed. At the corners, trim and tuck in the excess fabric to form a mitred seam. Press and ladder stitch or slip stitch the folded edges together.

EMBROIDERED BASKET

*Inspired by fond memories of 1950s raffia baskets, this design uses ribbon embroidery
to emblazon a plain shopping basket with a scattering of simple coloured daisies.*

YOU WILL NEED
paper for template
pencil
scissors
straw basket
fabric marker
large-eyed tapestry needle
narrow embroidery ribbons
needle and matching threads
matchstick

1 Copy the flower template at the back of the
  book and cut out.

2 Mark the design on the basket, turning the
  template through 180° for the second motif and
reversing it for the third.

3 Turn the template again for the fourth motif
  and return it to its original position for the fifth.
Repeat, changing the position of the flower, all
round the basket.

4 Mark a second row of flowers in the same way, turning and reversing the template to create the scattered flower design.

5 To embroider the stem, thread the tapestry needle with green ribbon. Knot the end and pull the ribbon through to the right side of the basket at one end of the stem. Insert the needle at the other end and pull the ribbon through to the wrong side. Tie a knot to finish off.

6 Thread a sewing needle with matching thread and couch sew the ribbon in place along the marked line.

7 To make the centre of the flower, thread the tapestry needle with a length of ribbon and make a small stitch over a matchstick. Do not pull the ribbon tight. Make a second small stitch over the matchstick and remove it. Work five more "knots" around the centre.

8 For the petals, thread the tapestry needle with ribbon and knot the end. Insert the needle on the wrong side and bring it out next to the centre knots. Insert the needle at the same point and return to the wrong side leaving a loop about 2.5 cm/1 in long.

9 Thread a sewing needle with matching thread and, bring-ing it out to the right side at the tip of the petal, sew down the loop. Repeat all round the flower. Continue stitching the flowers.

STRIPED CUSHION

Diagonal bands of satin, velvet and taffeta ribbon across this silk cushion make up a symphony of rich textures. Though all the tones are similar, light plays on the ribbons in different ways, making for dramatic contrasts. Feather-stitching along each band adds extra detail.

YOU WILL NEED
45 cm/18 in square silk fabric
tape measure
scissors
iron
selection of satin, velvet and taffeta ribbons
dressmaker's pins
needle and tacking (basting) thread
stranded embroidery cotton (floss) in complementary colours
20 x 40 cm/8 x 16 in velvet
sewing machine
matching thread
2 m/2¼ yd piping cord
40 cm/16 in zip (zipper)
stitch ripper
40 cm/16 in square cushion pad

1 For the cushion front, cut a 43.5 cm/17 in square from the silk fabric. Fold diagonally through the centre and press. Arrange lengths of ribbon side by side across the fabric, using the fold as a guide, and pin in place.

2 When you are satisfied with the ribbon positions, tack (baste) the ribbons to the front of the cushion.

3 Using stranded embroidery cotton (floss) in a range of colours to complement the ribbons, work rows of feather stitch to join the edges, varying the direction of the stitches.

4 Fold the velvet diagonally and cut 4 cm/1½ in wide strips parallel with the diagonal. Stitch the short edges together with a 5 mm/¼ in seam allowance and press open to make a length of bias binding. Pin the binding around the piping cord and machine stitch in place. ▶

5 Pin the covered cord all round the cushion front with the raw edges matching. Tack (baste) and machine stitch. Clip the seam allowance at the corners.

6 To join the piping, unpick 2 cm/¾ in of the machine stitching from the beginning of the piping. Trim away the cord so that the ends butt together and lap one end of the casing over the other, turning in the raw edges. Pin to the cover and machine stitch. Slip stitch the casing edge.

7 For the cushion back, cut two pieces of silk 23 x 43.5 cm/9 x 17 in. With right sides together, match the two long edges and machine stitch using a long stitch setting. Press the seam open, using a warm setting on the iron. Centre the zip (zipper) over the wrong side of the seam and tack in place.

8 Using a zipper foot on the sewing machine, top stitch all round the zip. Unpick the temporary seam carefully using a stitch ripper. Undo the zip. With right sides together, pin and machine stitch the cushion back and front together. Clip the corners, turn through and insert the cushion pad.

SHELF TRIMMING

Give added interest and charm to shelves displaying prized objects with some ribbon trimming in colours that enhance your collection. Pretty looped rosettes have been used here, together with a row of jaunty flags, like miniature bunting.

YOU WILL NEED
selection of wire-edged ribbons 50 mm/2 in and 25 mm/1 in wide
tape measure
scissors
satin ribbon to match the depth of the shelf fronts
dressmaker's pins
needle and matching thread
buttons
double-sided adhesive tape

1 To make the flag trimming, cut 10 cm/4 in lengths of two co-ordinating ribbons 50 mm/2 in wide. Cut the bottoms of one set of ribbons into fishtails.

2 Cut the bottoms of the other set into points.

3 Cut a length of satin ribbon to fit the shelf plus 2 cm/¾ in. Fold over the top edges of the flags and pin and hand stitch them, alternating the designs, along the ribbon.

4 To make a rosette, cut a piece of 25 mm/1 in ribbon 30 cm/12 in long. Make a loop with the first 8 cm/3¼in and secure with a stitch.

5 Make a second loop and secure, then make two more at right angles. Tuck in the raw ends.

6 Carefully gather up the ribbons in both directions at the centre. Secure with a pin.

7 Stitch a small button in the centre to hold the gathers in place.

8 Cut a piece of ribbon to fit the shelf as before. Stitch the rosettes at even intervals along its length. Attach the ribbons to the shelves using double-sided adhesive tape, turning in the raw edges at each end.

MATERIALS

*The materials needed for ribbonwork are available from good
department stores, craft shops and specialist ribbon shops.*

CHROME PIPE (1) Cut into short
lengths, chrome piping can be
suspended with narrow ribbons
from a wire ring to make the
chimes for a wind chime.

REEL WIRE (2) Thin florist's reel
wire is very useful for attaching
ribbon decorations, such as fixing
the tails to ribbon bows.

RIBBON
Grosgrain ribbon (3) is woven
to produce a distinctive ribbed
appearance. It is usually matt in
texture, and it is stronger and stiffer
than other ribbons. A range of
plain colours are available together
with woven striped patterns and
overprinted designs. Originally
produced for decorative use in
millinery, grosgrain ribbon is ideal
for a wide range of projects.
Jacquard ribbon (4) has patterns
woven into the ribbon, and it is
available in both solid colours and
multicoloured designs.
Satin ribbon (5) is a popular
choice for all manner of ribbon
projects because it is both attractive
and versatile. Satin ribbon is
available in many different widths
and colourways, both plain and
printed, and can be either single-
faced, that is shiny on one side, or
double-faced, shiny on both sides.

Sheer ribbon (6) is a delicate
and diaphanous ribbon, which is
available in plain colours and with
overprinted designs, satin stripes or
lurex threads.
Wire-edged ribbon (7) has fine
copper wire woven into or over-
locked on to both edges. It is ideal
for making decorative bows or gift
wrappings as the wire helps to
hold the shape. Wire-edged ribbon
can be plain or overprinted, and it
is available with satin or lurex
stripes, woven patterns or checks.

SMALL EGGS (8) Real blown birds'
eggs and painted plastic eggs make
effective decorative components.

TAPESTRY CANVAS (9) Stiff white
canvas can be used for templates
and to reinforce projects.

WADDING (BATTING) (10)
Polyester wadding (batting) is used
as a filling for quilting projects.

WIRE RING (11) Flush wire rings,
as used in lampshade-making, offer
lots of potential for ribbon projects.

WOODEN BALLS (12) Turned
wooden balls are available in
different sizes, with a hole drilled
through the centre. They make
useful decorative elements.

EQUIPMENT

There are few pieces of equipment needed for ribbonwork, and the most important are items commonly used for dressmaking.

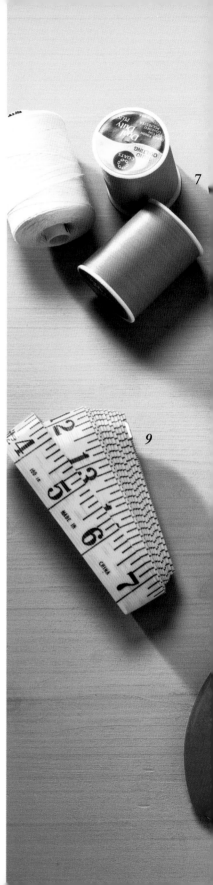

DRESSMAKER'S PINS (1) Fine steel dressmaker's pins are used to hold fabrics together, or to hold ribbon in place while tacking (basting), sewing or weaving.

HACKSAW (2) A small hacksaw is a useful tool to have available for cutting wooden battens or thin metal piping to size. A vice should be used to hold the batten or piping firmly in place as you cut.

NEEDLES (3) Hand-sewing needles are available in a range of sizes for all sewing purposes.

PENCIL (4) A soft pencil is useful for tracing around templates, and also for marking paper and canvas with sketched ideas for patterns and motifs to be embroidered.

RULER (5) A metal or plastic ruler is used for measuring length and for drawing straight lines when drafting patterns or templates.

SCISSORS (6) A good sharp pair of scissors that is comfortable to use is an invaluable tool. Medium-sized scissors can be used for general cutting out of fabric and trimming ribbons. A different pair of scissors should be used for cutting paper or cardboard.

SEWING THREADS (7) Synthetic, pure silk and cotton sewing threads are available in an extensive colour range for tacking (basting), hand or machine sewing and embroidery. For an extra decorative effect, choose threads woven with strands of gold.

TAILOR'S CHALK (8) This is used to mark out guidelines, templates or freehand patterns on ribbon or fabric. It is available in various colours, is non-staining and can easily be brushed away.

TAPE MEASURE (9) A flexible tape measure is useful for measuring curved lines or three-dimensional objects.

THIMBLE (10) Use a thimble to protect the tip of your finger when sewing, particularly when couching (sewing) ribbon to thick fabrics or when using narrow ribbons for embroidery.

BASIC TECHNIQUES

Ribbons are a supple and versatile material to work with, and as you handle the various types they will suggest ways in which you can use them decoratively. The techniques for making ornaments such as bows, roses and rosettes are simple to master.

SINGLE BOW

1 Cut a length of ribbon approximately four times the desired finished width of the bow. Lay the ribbon on your work surface and cross the ends over each other to form two loops.

2 Pinch the centre together with your fingers and hold the layers together firmly.

3 Take a short length of florist's reel wire and bind the bow tightly around the centre.

4 Fold the ends of the tails in half and snip diagonally with sharp scissors to form neat points.

MULTI-LOOP BOW

1 Cut a length of ribbon at least eight times the finished width of the bow, and fold it to form the number of loops required.

2 Bind the centre of the ribbon bow tightly with florist's reel wire.

3 Cut another length of ribbon and fold in half to find the centre. Bind to the bow with wire.

4 Take a short piece of ribbon, wrap it around the centre to cover the wire and then stitch the ends together neatly at the back of the bow using matching thread. Trim the ends of the bow into neat fishtails, if wished.

WEAVING RIBBON

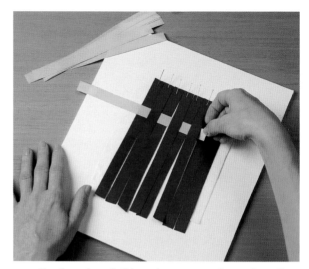

1 Cut a piece of iron-on interfacing to the finished size of the woven panel. Place the interfacing on a board with the adhesive side upwards. Cut lengths of ribbon approximately 5 cm/2 in longer than the finished panel to form the warp. Lay the warp pieces on the board and pin along the top edge only.

2 Cut lengths of ribbon in a contrasting colour for the weft, and weave the first row, passing the ribbon over one warp length and under the next until you reach the other side. Pin both ends to hold the ribbon in place.

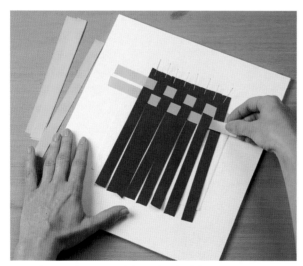

3 Weave the second length of ribbon under the first warp length and over the next, to make a plain checkered pattern. Pin both ends. Repeat this weaving pattern until the panel is complete.

4 Use a hot iron to press the woven panel, attaching the interfacing to the wrong side so that the pins can be removed.

APPLIQUE

1 Machine stitch down the centre of a length of satin ribbon with matching thread, using a long stitch setting. Gather the ribbon slightly along its entire length, gently pulling the bobbin thread.

2 Draw your design or motif on the fabric using tailor's chalk. The chalk marks can be brushed away afterwards.

3 Pin the gathered ribbon to the fabric following the chalked design lines, then use a hand running stitch and matching thread to secure the ribbon in place, stitching along the line of machine stitching.

SIMPLE RIBBON ROSE

1 Cut a 1 m/1 yd length of wide ribbon and fold one end at right angles, leaving a short "tail".

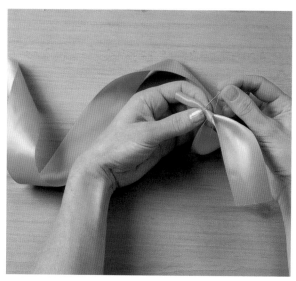

2 Make a few stitches using matching thread to hold the fold securely: this will form the centre of the rose.

3 Roll the ribbon around the tail a few times, then stitch in place at the base.

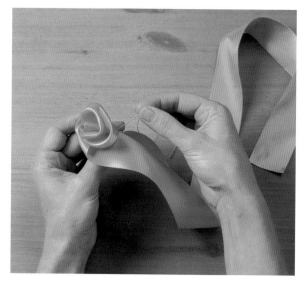

4 To form the petals, fold the ribbon over itself at right angles, then wrap it around the centre. Stitch in place at the base, then refold to make the next petal. Continue until the whole length of ribbon has been used. Stitch the raw end neatly to the base of the rose.

RUCHED RIBBON ROSE

1 Cut a 1 m/1 yd length of ribbon and fold one end at right angles to form a tail. Roll the ribbon around the tail a few times, then stitch securely at the base using matching thread.

2 Work a small running stitch along the lower edge of the ribbon, then gather up the ribbon and finish off the thread securely.

3 Wrap the gathered ribbon around the centre to form the rose.

4 Stitch the whole gathered edge of the ribbon securely at the base.

TEMPLATES

Enlarge the templates on a photocopier, or trace the design and draw a grid of evenly spaced

squares over your tracing. Draw a larger grid on to another piece of paper and copy the

outline square by square. Draw over the lines to make sure they are continuous.

Appliquéd Café Curtain, pp 56–59

Embroidered Basket, pp 72–74

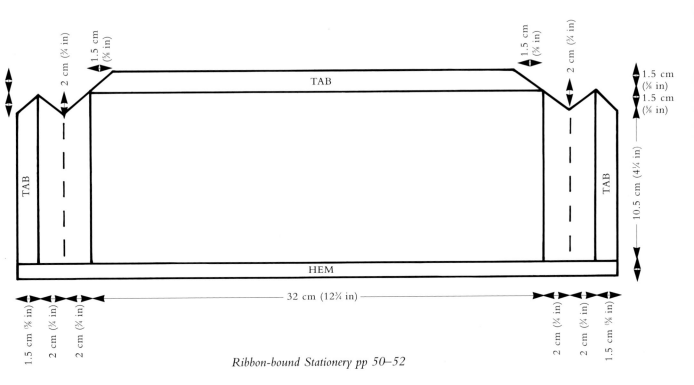

Ribbon-bound Stationery pp 50–52

SUPPLIERS

The materials and equipment required for the projects featured in this book can be found in large department stores and craft shops.

UNITED KINGDOM

C. M. Offrey & Sons Ltd
Fir Tree Place
Church Road
Ashford
Middlesex TW15 2PH
Tel: (0171) 631 3548

Clements of Watford
29 The Parade
Watford
Herts WD1 1LX
Tel: (01923) 244 222

Doughty Bros Ltd
33 Church Street
Hereford
Herefordshire HR1 2LL
Tel: (01432) 352 546

Fine Fabrics
Magdelene Lane
Taunton
Somerset TA1 1SE
Tel: (01823) 270 986

London Graphic Centre
16 Shelton Street
London WC2H 9JJ
Tel: (0171) 240 0095

Redburn Crafts
Squires Garden Centre
Halliford Road
Upper Halliford
Shepperton
Middlesex TW17 8RU
Tel (01932) 784 121

V. V. Rouleaux
10 Symons Street
London SW3 2TJ
Tel: (0171) 730 3125

UNITED STATES

Amster Ribbon & Novelty Co.
75-1371 Avenue
Middle Village
NY 11379
Tel: (718) 894-8660

C. M. Offrey & Son Inc.
Route 24
P. O. Box 601
Chester
NJ 07930-0601
Tel: (908) 879-4700

Guterman of America Inc.
P. O. Box 7387
Charlotte
NC 28241
Tel: (704) 525-7068

Victoria Faye
P. O. Box 640
Folsom
CA 95763
Tel: (916) 983-2321

CANADA
Abbey Arts & Crafts
4118 East Hastings Street
Vancouver, BC
Tel: (604) 299 5201

Dressew
337 W. Hastings Street
Vancouver, BC
Tel (604) 682 6196

**Michael's – The Arts & Craft
Superstore**
200 North Service Road
Oakville Town Center 2
Oakville
Ontario L6M 2VI
Tel: (905) 842 1555

AUSTRALIA
Beutron Australia Ltd
1 Queen Street
Auburn
NSW 2144
Tel: (02) 9649 2777

Spotlight
For your nearest branch contact
the head office, 100 Market Street,
South Melbourne, VIC 3205 or
telephone (03) 9690 8899.

NEW ZEALAND
Pan Pacific Marketing Ltd
38 Ronia Road
Mt Roskill
Auckland
Tel: (09) 629 3669

The Publishers would like to thank the following artists for the beautiful
projects shown in this book: Petra Boase: Easter Wreath, Faux Dado
(Chair) Rail, Rosy Lampshade; Penny Boylan: Tasselled Tie-back,
Rosette Picture Hanging, Pillowcase Edgings, Dressed-up Coat Hangers,
Christmas Decorations; Alison Jenkins: Special Occasion Table,
Ribbon Door Curtain, Woven Headboard, Ribbon Wind Chime,
Deck-chair Cover; Cheryl Owen: Ribbon-bound Stationery, Luxurious
Giftwrapping; Isabel Stanley: Trinket Bag, Appliquéd Café Curtain,
Linen Throw, Embroidered Basket, Striped Cushion, Shelf Trimming.

   Thanks are also due to Eva Ritchie and Tina Llomas for their help in
the studio, and to Elephant (0171 813 2093), Inventory (0171 937 2626),
Ever Trading (0181 878 4050) and Home Elements (0800 328 5351) for
furniture and accessories used in the photographs.

INDEX